HONOR **HB** BOOKS

Inspiration and Motivation for the Season of Life

An Imprint of Cook Communications Ministries • Colorado Springs, CO

Scripture quotations are taken from the *Holy Bible, New International Version*®. NIV®. Copyright © 1973, 1978, 1984 by International Bible Society. Used by permission of Zondervan Publishing House. All Rights reserved.

The Portable~Finding the Love of Your Life
ISBN 1-56292-558-X
Copyright © 2000 by Neil Clark Warren, Ph.D.
A Focus on the Family® book published by Honor Books, an imprint of
Cook Communications Ministries, Colorado Spring, Colorado 80918
Cook Communications, Paris, Ontario
Kingsway Communications, Eastbourne, England

5 6 7 8 9 10 11 12 13 14 Printing / Year 08 07 06 05 04

Printed in Canada. All rights reserved under International Copyright Law. Contents and/or cover may not be reproduced in whole or in part in any form without the expressed written consent of the Publisher.

Introduction

Every person I know yearns for love! The most obvious place to search for it is in marriage. In fact, more than 90 percent of all people in the United States will marry at least once during their lifetime.

A *Los Angeles Times* poll sampled the opinions of more than 2,000 American adults about their main goal in life. The overwhelmingly popular answer was "to be happily married." Marriage involves incredible potential for happiness. When two people "fall" in love and decide to spend the rest of their lives together, they can create unsurpassed joy for themselves and their children.

I am convinced that this life offers nothing comparable to the love of a man for his woman, and a woman for her man. When you find that true soul mate for whom you have longingly searched, you will be at the beginning of a relational journey filled with joy.

The discovery of a lifetime partner and lover is the closest thing possible to heaven on earth. To be loved forever by the person you most love is a God-given experience. It is in your pursuit of this kind of ecstasy—deep love within marriage—that I trust this book will be of value.

—Neil Clark Warren, Ph.D.

Table of Contents

Take Your Time Selecting a Mate

When deciding whether to marry someone, take your time. There's no rush! Longer courtships produce consistently healthier marriages. Many times couples will mistake physical attraction for the kind of love that can last a lifetime. Rather than examine their motivations, they rush into marriage with people they barely know.

A few years ago, an empirical study that underscores the importance of spending plenty of time together prior to marriage was published by researchers at Kansas State University. In their sample of fifty-one middle-aged wives, "a strong correlation was found between length of time spent dating their current spouses and current marital satisfaction."

ॐ

Therefore:

The chances of marital success are significantly increased by longer dating periods.

Grow Up First

Wait to get married until you know yourself well.
What are your goals in life? Do you want a full-
time career? Do you want a large family? Until you
know the kind of person with whom you can be
happy, wait to make the commitment of a lifetime.
It's too important a decision. This usually means
waiting until your mid-to-late twenties.

· ঌ

A recent study indicates that
the most stable marriages are forged by people
who are at least twenty-eight years of age when they marry.

ॐ

Therefore:

Take seriously the need to wait until you have personally
developed your identity and life goals. If you do, your selection
of a mate will be based on the "totally grown up you" and prove
to be as good ten or twenty years from now as it is today.

Play It Cool

When it comes to marriage, "cool your engines." Like any major decision that will affect the rest of your life, it always pays to think with your head as well as your heart. Make sure your mind is clear and settled with your choice. A lifetime decision, like marriage, requires an unhurried process of discovery about the other person.

ॐ

Therefore:

If it's true love, you'll both feel
the same way six months or a year from now.
The kind of love you need to carry you through
the circumstances of life will be more than
what's necessary for a Saturday-night date.
Make sure your choice for
a mate has "long-haul" potential.
A good marriage is worth the wait!

Please Yourself

You are the one who will live with your choice of
a mate for a lifetime. So please yourself, and pray
your choice will be pleasing to God.

Am I now trying to win the approval of men, or of God?
Or am I trying to please men?
If I were still trying to please men, I would not be a servant of Christ.

Galatians 1:10

Therefore:

To make a good decision,
make it in light of *your own*
needs, dreams, and life objectives—
not someone else's.
Long after your parents are gone and
your children have left for college,
you will still be married to your spouse.
That person should be your best friend
as well as your lover—a place of shelter
in the midst of the storm.

Take Her Out to the Ball Game

A change of scenery can tell you volumes about another person. Do you normally just go to the movies on a date? Then how about buying tickets to an afternoon baseball game. Do you always eat at the same fast-food place? Then how about dressing up and going out to dinner in a fancy restaurant. You can make a far more accurate prediction about how much you will enjoy being married to a person if your experience together is more varied.

૱

Therefore:

It's crucial to broaden your experiences
together as much as possible.
Spend time with your spouse-to-be
early in the morning and late at night,
in heavy traffic and on country roads,
in times of stress and easygoing moments.
Observe him or her playing with children,
doing household chores, and balancing
the checkbook. The more experiences
you share together, the better are your chances
of avoiding hidden surprises later on in life.

Get Real

Give your expectations of marriage a reality check. Marriage is a mixed bouquet of roses, daisies, and wildflowers. The marriage vows call for standing by the one you love in sickness and in health, in bad times and in good. Being committed to sticking together no matter what the circumstances is crucial to a successful marriage. Remember, you choose your attitude.

"**If** we focus only on the loving side of a relationship, we may become caught in the 'bliss trap'—imagining that love is a stairway to heaven that will allow us to rise above the nitty-gritty elements of our personality and leave behind all our fears and limitations. . . . Inevitably [we must] return to earth and . . . deal with the real-life challenges of *making a relationship work.*"

—John Welwood

ॐ

Therefore:

Be realistic about your expectations.

If Your Favorite Flower Is an Orchid, Don't Marry a Rose with Thorns

Remember the last time you tried to change someone else's personality? Remember the last time someone tried to change yours? God gifted each of us with our own special temperament. Some people are easygoing; others are high-strung. When you marry someone, you marry his or her disposition. Marriage may soften our rough edges, but it won't change our basic personality.

Therefore:

Decide now if you can live
with that person's idiosyncrasies for a lifetime.
Ask yourself, *Is my potential life mate
always dependable, truthful, and happy?
If not, do I want to live with someone of
that type of temperament for the rest of my life?
Can I build trust with this person?*
Address and overcome those differences
now . . . before you're married.

How Do We Form the Image of a Perfect Mate?

There are many theories floating around about how we're influenced to marry a particular type of person. One theory says that the perfect mate in our heads is like our parent of the opposite sex. However, there is very little research supporting this theory.

Another theory says that the image of our perfect mate is fueled by unmet childhood needs from the opposite-sex parent. This assumption is also with little foundation.

చ

The theory I favor is that every child is influenced by countless persons, and each helps shape the image of your desired mate. Your parents, relatives, teachers, coaches, and others all had certain qualities you found attractive. Each of these qualities became a piece of the puzzle in the formation of your perfect spouse image.

Therefore:

Consider all the people in your life who have influenced you positively, and ask yourself what traits in them you most admire.

Develop a Clear Mental Picture of "Mr." or "Mrs. Right"

A monumental decision like marriage deserves highly precise reasoning. It's crucial to make a rational, proactive, fully conscious decision about the type of person you want to marry. Moonbeams and stardust are wonderfully exciting and romantic, but we need a little sunshine every day to keep us on the right track. Is your spouse-to-be a "light on the hill" or only a dim reflection?

Therefore:

Daydream a little and form
a clear picture of your perfect mate.
Put your pen to paper and list all those traits you
would like in a spouse. Get specific. Start with
temperament, and even write down physical
appearance. If you're already considering marriage to
someone, compare that person to your perfect image
of a mate. Is there a match? If not, it's time to
question your choice.

Traits to Consider

There are ten general areas that are important to consider when formulating the image of your ideal spouse. You may choose to add to this list, but these are the dimensions most often considered. Got your pen and paper ready? It's time to start making notes as you read about the following criteria to help choose a mate.

Personality

What type of personality do you want in a future mate? Here are five questions to ask yourself:

1. Would you like your mate to be quiet or talkative?

2. Do you prefer people who are intense or laid-back?

3. Are you most drawn to people who are funny or serious?

4. Would you like someone who is independent or someone who leaves the decision-making up to you?

5. Do you prefer softness and gentleness or tough straight-talk?

Intelligence

People possess various *types* of intelligence as well as various *degrees* of intelligence. Figure out the level and type of intelligence you want your mate to possess.

༈

Did You Know?

Recent studies indicate that in stable marriages there is a high correlation in intelligence. Couples do best when they are matched with someone of a similar IQ—whether geniuses, above average, or average.

- What *kind* of intelligence would you like in your mate—analytical or intuitive?

- Do you prefer a "thinker" or a "feeler"?

- Do you like to go to movies with someone who analyzes what the movie was trying to say or someone who talks about how the movie made him or her feel?

Appearance

While it would be foolish to base your decision too heavily on appearance, your individual tastes should be considered when formulating the image of your perfect mate. You must settle on your own preferences regarding height, weight, facial appearance, hair color, style of dress, cleanliness, and physical movement.

ॐ

Ambition

It's fine if two people want carefree, relaxing lives. *But they need to be in agreement about their goals.* On the other hand, if they want a big house, expensive cars, and international trips, they both need to agree on the career styles that will accommodate those aims. When their levels of ambition are similar, it can bond them together as they strive to reach their goals and achieve their dreams.

Chemistry

A strong mutual attraction—chemistry—is critical
for long-term satisfaction in marriage.

ॐ

Questions to Consider:

- Is the magic of romance important to you, or are you content to make a logical decision based on sound reasoning?

- How much emphasis do you place on romance and physical attraction?

- Is chemistry an essential factor in the selection of your mate?

- Is it a major part of the image you have of your perfect person?

Spirituality

Religion often refers to *externals*—which church you attend, what denomination you're affiliated with, what traditions you follow. Spirituality refers to *internal* faith and beliefs that run deep. Have you asked your potential mate about his or her belief system? Consider attending worship services together, and then discuss your thoughts and impressions.

ॐ

Did You Know?

Research consistently has shown that religious commitment and marital success are highly related. Married couples who regularly attend worship services generally are happier.

Character

Our unique character traits distinguish us as distinct individuals in a world of an infinite number and variety of people types. We are made up of a combination of mental, spiritual, and emotional qualities that can be strengthened and built up by making the right choices in our life experiences. Sturdiness, resilience, and consistency of character are fundamental prerequisites for a stable, long-lasting, and joyful marriage.

※

- How important is it to you that your mate be absolutely trustworthy?

- How much do you want to be married to someone who operates on the basis of strongly-held values and acts with courage, even when it requires sacrifice?

- How much do you need a mate who absolutely will not cheat for any reason?

- How crucial is it that your mate would never steal, act irresponsibly, or take drugs?

Creativity

Writers, artists, poets, and musicians aren't the only types of people who express creativity. Abraham Maslow, a great American psychologist, pointed out that creativity happens most often among ordinary folks—people just like you and me. When genuine love is mixed with creativity, lovers can fully celebrate and enjoy their life together.

ॐ

- How would you feel about your mate being a good mother but a poor housekeeper?
- How would you feel if your spouse-to-be was creative but fell a little short in other ways?

Parenting

Is it important to you that your mate be interested in raising children? If so, you may want to observe your future spouse with younger sisters and brothers, nieces and nephews, or with other children. See if you are comfortable and attracted to the parenting tendencies exhibited. If you desire to have a family, finding a mate who shares that goal will make your life significantly more rewarding.

୬

Authenticity

Many people wear masks in social situations. They put their best foot forward at a party or in the workplace, but at home, they are totally different people. Authenticity is the ability to be completely yourself—to be forthright with your opinions and comfortable with who you are. Examine your own personality. Are you an authentic person? Does your potential mate know the real you?

ॐ

Questions to Consider:

- How important is it that your mate be authentic?

- Would you be willing to let that person be who he or she really is, especially if that freedom could cause disagreement?

- What personality traits are essential to you?

- Are you willing to compromise on the type of person you desire?

Therefore:

Formulate a clear, *truthful* picture of the ideal person with whom you would like to spend the rest of your life.

Find a Person to Love Who Is a Lot Like You

Research findings are highly consistent:

The most stable marriages are those involving two people with many similarities. What similarities are most critical for marital happiness? All similarities are assets. But there are some that are incredibly strengthening to a relationship and contribute to the overall health of a marriage.

॰ॐ॰

Intelligence

If both individuals are similarly endowed intellectually, the marriage seems to have considerably less strain. Research indicates that when IQ scores are within the same general range, stability in marriage is much more likely. It doesn't matter so much *how smart* the partners are, but it does matter *how close* they are intellectually. Individuals of similar intelligence are able to communicate and understand one another more fully.

ॐ

Values

There are dozens of values on which couples need to agree. For instance, it's a real asset when two people place a similar importance on spiritual pursuits or family life. If they both love to attend church, Bible studies, and prayer sessions, their spiritual bond and level of happiness will be enhanced. This is a strong, fundamental issue that will cause great joy in a relationship.

৯৫

Verbal Intimacy

When both people deeply enjoy sharing their lives fully, they have an asset that will help them overcome any differences throughout their lives. Communicating at a deeper level than just everyday chatter will create an intimacy in all areas of life. Couples who share their dreams, goals, and joys and who consistently encourage one another have a treasure money can't buy.

ॐ

Interests

When there are several things two people enjoy doing together, they have a large field on which they can happily play the game of life. It is always best if these interests are a combination of physical, mental, and spiritual pursuits. It's most beneficial to a relationship if the couple enjoys similar music, games, sports, theater, and reading material. Ask yourself whether you and your potential mate limit your recreational time together or whether you pursue a variety of activities.

ॐ

Role Expectations

When a man and a woman have compatible ideas about duties and responsibilities in the relationship and household, it is cause for celebration. It is essential to talk about your expectations before considering marriage.

ॐ

Questions to Consider:

- Do you have a traditional view of the male/female roles in the home?
- Do you have a nontraditional view of marriage roles?
- Is your idea of an equal partnership in marriage equivalent to an equal division of all the household chores?

Differences to Consider

Energy Level

Different people have different energy levels. This energy discrepancy may surface in almost any area of life. Stop to consider how similar you are to your spouse-to-be in this area.

ॐ

<u>Questions to Consider:</u>

- After marriage, will you hop out of bed early each morning, ready to tackle your to-do list, while your mate snoozes until ten o'clock?
- Do you like to be on the go all the time? Or do you enjoy a more leisurely pace?
- Do you and your potential marriage partner have the same amount of "get-up-and-go"?

Personal Habits

For a more satisfying union, consider the following habits and how compatible you are with your potential mate: punctuality, cleanliness, orderliness, dependability, responsibility, and weight management.

༜

Questions to Consider:

- *Are you always on time for an appointment, or are you consistently late?*
- *Is your potential mate a meticulous housekeeper, or is that person messy?*
- *Do you enjoy rich chocolate cheesecake, or are you always on a diet?*

Use of Money

Both parties need to agree on the handling of their finances. Explore this area carefully *before* marriage.

ॐ

- Do you want to save money for the future or spend money and enjoy life to the fullest now?

- Do you want to take risks to multiply your savings, or would you rather invest slowly and surely?

- Are you generous with charities, or do you want to save for your future only?

Verbal Skills and Interests

Couples who enjoy the same amount of conversation will be more likely to feel a high level of comfort in the relationship.

༄

Questions to Consider:

- Does your potential mate talk a lot or very little?
- Do you need a lot of time alone to "recharge your battery"?
- Do you like to talk about every detail of your life?

*"Successful human mating follows
the line of genetic similarity."*
—J. Phillippe Rushton

ॐ

Therefore:

Stable and satisfying marriages
usually involve two people
who are very much alike in
many areas of their lives.

Get Yourself Healthy Before You Get Yourself Married

A great marriage requires two healthy people, and the time to get healthy is before you get married. I'm not talking about physical health, although it is important. And I'm not talking about spiritual health, although successful relationships are spiritually vital. Strong *emotional* and *mental* health contributes significantly to marital strength and happiness.

Emotional Issues

Managing Your Internal "Heat"

There are many emotional issues that must be dealt with to build a solid and successful marriage. The ability to handle your emotions effectively is one of the key issues.

<u>Questions to Consider:</u>

- How does your potential mate channel irritation over small matters?
- Do you explode when circumstances don't go your way?
- Do you and your potential mate argue a lot, or do you agree on most issues?

Marriage Is a "Two-way Street"

Instead of someone who has an excessive admiration of his- or herself, look for someone with a more caring nature . . . someone who will care about you—about your feelings and your needs. Marriage is a "two-way street," and if you both give 100 percent to the other, you will both come out on top as winners!

Ambrose Bierce once defined marriage as "the state or condition of a community consisting of a master, mistress, and two slaves, making in all, two."

ॐ

Therefore:

Marriage partners must serve each other.
There will be times when one spouse is weaker and
will need more care, and the roles may switch next year,
depending on the circumstances. Learn to be a giver!

Personality Disturbances

If you discover that your potential mate suffers from depression, moodiness, or temper tantrums, suggest he or she seek professional help. Sometimes these conditions can be effectively treated with prescribed medication or through wise counsel. The dating period is the best time to face these issues, while you can still decide whether you want to pursue the relationship.

Dependencies

A chemical or emotional dependency affects your health, work, and primary relationships. Again, these are issues which need to be treated and resolved *before* marriage. You may decide to stick with an individual through treatment, or you may decide to walk away. But you will have the satisfaction of being able to make an informed choice.

ॐ

Parental Issues

Our mothers and fathers are the most important developmental influences in our lives. We learn thousands of things from them during our childhood years and even later. Find out about your potential mate's early home life. What were his or her parents like? It will help you to understand your potential spouse's personality.

"A child's success at feeling both distinct from and connected to its mother has a profound impact on all later relationships."
—Harville Hendrix

Therefore:

Upon entering marriage, an ideal relationship
with our parents would be one in which:

- We are emotionally independent individuals.

- We are clear about what is true of our
  relationships with our mother and father, and
  what is true in relation to our spouse.

- We have established a relationship with our
  parents in which they will not intrude in our
  marriage, and yet we can still maintain a
  closeness and connectedness to them.

What Makes Us Healthy People?

Inner Security

There is a kind of inner security and peace in healthy people. They are not always thinking that their worth as a person is on the line, or that they always have to be right in order to be accepted and valued. Healthy people respect themselves and others. They know how to laugh at themselves. Do you and your future marriage partner have this kind of deep down security?

ॐ

Respect for the Truth

A healthy person has an enormous respect for the truth. Truth is always based on eternal values and absolutes. It is the guiding force behind all of our decisions—from big matters, like whom we will marry, to little matters, like which television program we will watch right now. The truth may be hard to discern sometimes, but a healthy person tries to get as close to it as possible.

ॐ

Collecting All the Information

Healthy people also know that the best way to discern truth is by collecting all the information and allowing all the facts to be shared. They listen carefully and want to know what you really think about an issue. They respect your opinion even though they may not agree with you. They celebrate the differences between people.

ॐ

Weighing the Information

Healthy people weigh the information they collect. They place different values on various parts of the information through the use of careful, although usually unconscious, internal processes. These thought processes are deeply influenced by well-established moral codes—a value system that influences all decision making. They filter the information through their value system and are able to see gray areas as well as black and white.

৯৯

Authenticity

Healthy people are authentic. They stand in the middle of all the information they've collected and come to a decision that is closest to the truth. With courage and total commitment, they state that position as honestly as they know how and live in accordance with it until they change in light of some new information. They have a deep humility that seems to emanate from their recognition that they are fallible human beings.

ॐ

How to Get Healthy

Look for Unconditional Love

Find a source of unconditional love. God is the best source of love you'll ever find! But when you find someone who will love you with the love of God, you have found a treasure. Does your potential mate give you this kind of love?

ॐ

How great is the love the Father has lavished on us,
that we should be called children of God!

1 John 3:1

Love Yourself

Learn to love yourself. It isn't enough that someone else loves you, even if that someone is God. You have to accept the fact that you are lovable. When you do, you'll discover you don't have to fabricate yourself in order to please someone else and earn his or her love. You can just be the authentic you, the real you who is special and unique.

ॐ

Look for a Friend

Find someone to encourage, inspire, and challenge you. We all need close friends, because it's hard for us to understand our emotions and know exactly what we're feeling and thinking deep within. We need someone to help us sort through our thoughts and feelings and confront our problems. There's no better person to fill this role than your spouse.

ॐ

As iron sharpens iron, so one man sharpens another.
Proverbs 27:17

Support

Cultivate relationships with people who will help you take a stand, be authentic, and feel secure in your position. We all need people who will stay with us, cheer us on, bolster our shaky confidence, and reinforce our courage. An ongoing support system helps us stay on track, even when we feel like falling back into unhealthy patterns. Man was not meant to go through life alone. God made us social beings, and we need the love and support of one another.

ॐ

Therefore:

Regardless of the method you choose,
it is essential for you to become an
emotionally healthy person prior to marriage.
In fact, the healthier you are, the healthier
your marriage will be. As you search for a mate,
look for the traits of a healthy person.

Find a Love You Can Feel Deep in Your Heart

Someone once said, "Love is only for the young, the middle-aged, and the old."

For everyone, love is a powerful force that energizes our lives and revolutionizes our relationships. Love can transform momentary struggles into compelling adventures. It can marvelously change hard work into wonderful opportunities. It can motivate courageous behavior. Love is the greatest thing in the world. It deserves our deepest respect and appreciation.

ॐ

"Someday after we have mastered the air, the winds, the tides, and gravity, we will harness for good the energies of love. And then for the second time in the history of the world, man will have discovered fire."
—Pierre Teilhard de Chardin

ॐ

Therefore:

When two people are in love, they want to be with each other all the time. All of this "togetherness" is designed to introduce them to one another, helping them to steadily progress toward deeper levels of intimacy.

"Brevity may be the soul of wit but not
when someone's saying 'I love you.'
When someone's saying 'I love you,'
he always ought to give a lot of details:
like, why does he love you?
And, how much does he love you? . . .
Favorable comparisons with all other
women he ever loved are welcome,
and even though he insists it would take
forever to count the ways in which he loves you,
you wouldn't want to discourage him. . . ."

—Judith Viorst

Therefore:

During this stage of blissful happiness
and contentment, there may not be
enough words to say how you feel.
Some people express themselves better face
to face; others may be better at telling you
how much they love you in a letter.
Regardless, we need to communicate
our devotion to our loved one.
How else will that person know we care?

ॐ

What Causes Two People to Be Attracted to One Another?

I doubt research will ever fully explain why two
people "fall" in love. But I have a theory: I believe
initial attraction is a match between a real person
and a "dreamed-about person." Part of this dream
involves physical characteristics—body shape,
facial appearance, smell, skin texture, and hair
color. Sometimes the match occurs on the basis of
appearance alone, but for others, it becomes
obvious only when they touch. For still others, it
takes a while, after the two people have gotten to
know each other.

৵

The Purpose Behind the Passion

Passionate love performs a powerful service, as long as it lasts. It focuses the total attention of two people on each other long enough for them to build an enduring relationship. That's another function of passionate love—the life-changing experience of being accepted and valued. Passionate love shines a bright, positive light on each of the persons involved, and both of them "fall" in love not only with each other but also with themselves.

ॐ

Did You Know?

Psychologists Ellen Berscheid and Elaine Walster
have concluded that attraction occurs
when we believe that others:

- like us.

- have highly similar views to our own political, social,
  economic, and religious issues.

- are eager to support us if we are lonely, fearful, or under
  stress.

"Love cures people—both the ones who give it and the ones who receive it."
—Dr. Karl Menninger

ॐ

Therefore:

If someone we respect and value feels good about us,
our most pressing emotional quest will be satisfied.
It makes us happy when our love is returned by the one we love.
Mutual admiration is a balm to the soul.

Passionate Love Can Make or Break a Relationship

God's invention of passionate love is one of the most magnificent parts of His creation. But in the early phases of a relationship, great care must be given to the expression of these feelings. There are logical steps for falling more deeply in love. Never jump to the last stage of a relationship if you are still early in the love process.

రిశ

Principles for Expressing Passionate Love

- Passionate love between two people is a crucial ingredient if they are to have a long and satisfying relationship.

- Passionate love always involves strong physical attraction. A lack of affection or desire for physical intimacy should raise a red flag in your mind. But physical involvement must be managed with extreme care. Strongly defined boundaries need to be agreed upon, and there has to be self-discipline exerted to stay within those limits.

ॐ

· *Every progression of physical activity establishes a new plateau—and it is extremely difficult to retreat once the next level has been reached.*

· *When sexual expression is not kept in check, the emotional, cognitive, and spiritual aspects of the relationship become slaves to the physical desires.*

ॐ

Physical attraction is critical, but it needs to develop in correlation with other parts of the relationship.

Therefore:

Love is experienced in the heart, but
the decision about marriage is carefully
protected until the moment that
permanent commitment is pledged.
If both of these goals are reached,
love can flourish in a marriage
that will last a lifetime.

Let Passionate Love Mature Before You Decide to Marry

There is a necessary transition from "passionate love" to what is sometimes called "companionate love." Professor Bernard Murstein describes this latter kind of love this way: "Companionate love . . . may be defined as a strong bond, including tender attachment, enjoyment of the other's company, and friendship. . . . The main difference between passionate and companionate love is that . . . the latter thrives on contact and requires time to develop and mature."

<u>Questions to Consider</u>

- Am I addicted to the excitement that is present in the early phases of passionate love?

- Do I want to move on to the next stage of companionate love?

- Could this person become the "best friend of my life" as well as the "love of my life"?

- Will I be able to develop and sustain a deep friendship even when the ecstatic feelings of passionate love fade?

- How do I know when I'm ready to move toward a deeper relationship?

Therefore:

Sometimes passionate love fails to develop
into a deeper love because one or both people
recognize their relationship is "just not right."
When this happens, the dating process has worked.
It's better to recognize that the person you've been
dating is not the person you want to marry than to
marry him or her and then discover your error.

How to Recognize a Wrong Relationship

There are countless reasons why you might be tempted to perpetuate a relationship that should have ended at an early stage. Perhaps you feel that you may not find anyone else as good or better. Or you may think that if you just try harder, the relationship might work out. Perhaps you don't want to hurt the other person or worry that you might regret your decision later.

ॐ

Are you letting fantasy triumph over fact?

Remember, the other person deserves someone

who will love them unconditionally. If you have

misgivings, if your love is superficial and

inadequate, then you need to let them go.

Therefore:

You may know that happiness requires a definite decision and no fence-sitting.
But perhaps you find yourself frightened to tell another person that this
relationship just isn't right for you. Remember, until you let go,
God cannot bring the right person into your life.

What Does Companionate Love Look Like?

Unselfish Commitment

*"Love begins when a person finds another
person's needs to be as important as his own."*
—Harry Stack Sullivan

ॐ

Companionate love gives itself unconditionally.
The other person's needs are crucial to you.
Enduring love involves an unselfish commitment
to your lover's happiness.

Common Interests

Companionate love helps you enjoy what your marriage partner enjoys. I used to puzzle over the fact that some couples seem to have so many interests in common, while others have so few. In time, however, I've discovered that few couples share these interests naturally. Rather, they develop them together. They love each other so much that they start enjoying what their lover enjoys.

ॐ

Individual Interests

People who love each other deeply recognize the value of developing three spaces in their relationship—one for him, one for her, and one for them. This may seem contradictory, but it really isn't. Common interests are important, but equally important are individual interests. Separate hobbies for both persons provide opportunities to gain experiences and refresh themselves. When they come together, they have more to offer each other.

ॐ

Quietness and Solitude

People who love each other in a mature and enduring way seem to recognize the importance of finding individual wholeness, and they know this usually comes during periods of quietness and solitude.

ॐ

"A good marriage is that in which each appoints the other guardian of his solitude. Once the realization is accepted that even between the closest human beings infinite distances continue to exist, a wonderful living side-by-side can grow up. . . ."
—Rainer Maria Rilke

Freedom to Share Yourself

Genuine love provides the freedom to share your real self with your spouse. It is in the sharing of the deepest and most central parts of ourselves that we allow another person to really know us. The more we are known, the more we can be loved. If only superficial things are known about us, we will be loved only superficially.

ॐ

Trust

Companionate love requires trust, and trust requires trustworthiness. There are several aspects to relational trust. First, we need to trust our mate to be genuinely interested in us—in our safety and growth and success. Second, we need to trust that our mate will keep promises and avoid compromises that would damage the relationship. And third, becoming trustworthy requires unconditional love. It is this level of trust that makes for generous and genuine love that will withstand the test of time.

༃

Dream Together

Couples who dream great dreams together tend to love each other more. Shared dreams have a way of cementing two people together.

ॐ

<u>Did You Know?</u>

In 1990, the Roper Institute surveyed 3,000 women and 1,000 men selected randomly from across America. These people were asked, "What makes a good marriage?" Out of all the answers given, one was most common for both sexes. "Being in love" was the answer given by 87 percent of the women and 84 percent of the men.

Developing Companionate Love

Companionate love involves two people who know how to focus specifically on each other, listen long and carefully, and understand one another on a deep level. They discover each other's internal worlds, and they learn to love each other for qualities that are basically unchanging. They overlook defects and focus on attributes. Finally, they go to work in an effort to help each other solve problems and reach goals. This is what it means to be "in love."

ॐ

Therefore:

It is clear that being "in love" involves
significantly more than passion and romance.
It is the deep, woven-together quality of two people
who have developed a many-sided relationship.
These people know they are cherished and
honored and loved by their marriage partner.

ॐ

Master the Art of Intimacy

Without question, the most important quality in a great marriage is intimacy. Intimacy is to romance what April showers and May sunshine are to a farmer's crops. When two people come to know one another deeply, they can truly become what the Bible calls "one flesh."

⋰

*For this reason a man will leave his father and mother
and be united to his wife, and they will become one flesh.*
Genesis 2:24

Teaching Children Verbal Intimacy

Intimacy is a skill that families should teach their children during the developmental years. Life is so fast-paced that there isn't much opportunity to sit down for long periods and communicate. Most individuals don't have time to figure out what's really going on inside themselves, let alone take time to share it with others. Yet the family is the best place to teach a child how to communicate on a deep level and build lasting relationships with other people.

ॐ

Reinforcing Truthful Communication

Our society needs to reward and reinforce those who master the art of communication. People are paid more in our society if they produce well; given prestige if they pursue higher education; and deemed valuable if they look good. But people who are able to communicate intimately with others are given little special recognition. We can make a difference by recognizing those who communicate truthfully and encouraging them in their behavior.

Exploring Our Inner World

Intimacy requires a careful exploration of one's own inner world. In our country there has been an epidemic of inattentiveness to the authentic inner self. Intimacy is made possible by self-exploration, coming to understand one's own personality, dreams, and desires. It is a skill which needs to be communicated and taught to others. All of us need to know ourselves well to communicate well with others. Do you and your lover understand yourselves at this deep level?

ॐ

Learning to Be More Intimate

Psychotherapy involves intimacy—the discovery of oneself in the context of a meaningful relationship with a trusted guide. A skilled therapist or counselor can uncover roadblocks to intimacy and provide a safe environment for self-discovery.

Others may benefit from a therapy group. These groups allow members to relive family situations and discuss their daily interactions. Fellow group members serve as a mirror, reflecting back what they see to help clarify thoughts and behaviors.

ॐ

Twelve-step programs or church groups that emphasize growth and self-understanding may help some individuals. These are geared for people with similar problems, and there is often strong accountability and encouragement.

Another wonderful self-discovery exercise is keeping a daily journal; write out your feelings and thoughts for a half-hour each day, schedule times of reflection and prayer, and discuss new insights with your potential spouse. This "mind and spirit homework" helps uncover memories, sort out thoughts, and explore feelings.

ॐ

Conditions That Foster Intimacy

Interest

People must be assured you really want to hear
from them. If you don't, you won't need to say so.
It will become evident very quickly.

Commitment

The deepest kind of sharing can take place only
when there's no fear of rejection or abandonment.
When true commitment exists, both persons feel
free to dialogue about anything and everything.

Camaraderie

People who reveal their emotions need to
know you genuinely like them. Only then can
they open up their heart to you.

ॐ

Participation

Persons who genuinely love each other and seek a
deep relationship actively participate in the intimacy
process. They sit forward, maintain eye contact, ask
probing questions, and guide the discussion with
comments. Intimacy is nurtured when two people
listen carefully to each other, convey their support to
one another, and refrain from judging and blaming.

Shared Emotions and Experiences

Intimacy is impossible without at least a thread of shared emotions, experiences, or beliefs. The more commonalities there are, the deeper intimacy can go. Mutually held spiritual beliefs promote deep intimacy in a relationship. Asking questions and being truly interested in a person's responses will signal that it's safe to share at a deeper level.

৩৯

<u>Did You Know?</u>

One research study showed that spirituality ranked
among the six most common characteristics of strong families.
The strongest families in this study reported experiencing
"a sense of power and a purpose"
greater than themselves—*a spiritual orientation.*

When Is Intimacy Most Likely to Occur?

Time Is Crucial

Research studies indicate that marital happiness is highly correlated with the amount of time spent together. Even taking a leisurely stroll contributes to intimacy. Today many couples find themselves working long hours and struggling to keep up with the demands of life, and there is little time to talk about the feelings and experiences that matter most. We all need to make more time to enjoy our spouses and families.

ॐ

Escape from Routine

Intimacy often gets crowded out by day-to-day duties and distractions. There is something about the home and office grind that switches our brains to an action mode, often thwarting introspection. Escape from that routine, and you will begin to relax and open your mind. It may be just a dinner across town or a drive to the country or an hour at the park. These "time outs" make intimacy possible to achieve.

ॐ

In Crisis or Pain

When we are in emotional or physical pain, we turn inward and examine what we feel and think. When we discover what's going on inside of us, we want to tell the people we love most. Even those who have little awareness of their internal processes are often willing to share their thoughts and feelings when faced with a crisis or tragedy.

ॐ

Reflection and Introspection

Time alone to read and think, to ponder and
pray, nearly always leads to deeper awareness.
Couples who have a regular time of reflection
excel at intimacy. If you get more deeply in touch
with yourself, you always have more to give to the
intimacy process. Rather than replacing intimate
time with your spouse, it actually enhances your
time when you do get together for conversation.

ॐ

Therefore:

Intimacy helps you assess your relationship.
It does not *automatically* contribute to
bonding and connectedness. When you are
intimate with another person, you are sharing
your innermost world, and in this process,
you become deeply known to each other.
This awareness will either confirm
a sense of oneness or highlight
differences and separateness.

ॐ

Learn How to Clear Conflict from the "Road of Love"

Disagreements and quarrels in a relationship are inevitable, and if approached with openness and respect, they can be beneficial. If two people know how to resolve conflicts so that their relationship deepens and matures, they possess a magnificent skill. Rather than fostering silent resentment, the conflict can be aired openly and resolved, leaving the couple free to face together whatever challenges life may offer around the next bend of the road.

ॐ

Conflict Can Contribute to a Strong Marriage

The degree to which any couple can allow for openness and authenticity is the degree to which their relationship will be complete and satisfying. If they hide their thoughts and feelings out of fear that conflict may result, it won't be long until they feel a sense of inner lostness and resentment toward each other. Conflict that is resolved in a healthy way helps to clear up misunderstandings or miscommunication.

ॐ

Good relationships allow for a considerable amount of individual freedom for one of two reasons. Two people may discover in their openness that they are very much alike, perhaps because of cultural and genetic similarities. Or they may discover that the two of them, even though they have differences, have learned to manage these differences to the ultimate advantage of their relationship. It is this skill that every couple needs to develop before they marry.

ॐ

The Secret of Successful Conflict Resolution

Constructive conflict revolves around mutual respect and concern for the other person's individual needs. If you respect yourself and the other person, you will check inside yourself for the answer to an important question and then take your time in formulating this answer. You will be satisfied with your answer, and you will state your opinions with assurance. If this is true for you, then most likely you have individual and collective trust and respect.

৯৹

How can you tell whether your potential mate respects you? Watch the person while you are talking to see how much attention he or she pays to you. Observe facial expressions and the amount of eye contact that is maintained. Conflict is a thousand times easier to manage if two people deeply respect themselves and each other. If that foundation is present, the techniques of conflict resolution can be learned easily.

ॐ

Proven Ways to Resolve Conflict

Agree to Disagree

In conflict resolution, there must be a basic agreement that both people have a legitimate right to feel and think the way they do. No one is wrong simply because he or she disagrees with the other person or does things differently. It's okay to have a different point of view.

Listen

Both persons need to be fully heard by their partner, and they need to know they have been accurately understood. For most people, it's more important to be heard and understood than to win a point. If you know that the other person understands your thoughts and feelings, you automatically feel relieved, even if your differences continue. Now you're ready for the next skill.

ॐ

Define the Conflict

Your points of disagreement need to be specified carefully and then agreed upon.

It can be hard to define the problem, so sometimes it is best to do this in writing. By doing this, you clear away any confusion and identify the root issues. Then you're ready for the next skill.

ॐ

Compromise

An attitude of "give and take" greatly facilitates conflict resolution. You need to say something like this to each other: "Where can I give and where can you give so we can move toward one another?" When two people make a move to compromise with each other, they are on the threshold of actually benefiting from their conflict.

ॐ

Congratulations

When you resolve a conflict with your possible marriage partner, congratulate each other. Praise the person you love for the qualities that allowed both of you to get your needs met and feel important in the process. This allows for a "win-win" situation and builds a deeper intimacy.

જ

Methods to Avoid in Conflict Resolution

Denial

Some people are so convinced that conflict is destructive that they refuse to even acknowledge it in themselves. They deny that anything is wrong. Remember, healthy people are able to engage in conflict and still love and respect themselves and the other person. If conflict is a difficult problem for you, and if a relationship is worth saving, seek wise counsel on how to manage your disagreements.

ॐ

Non-engagement

Some people simply will not engage in conflict, but they will let their displeasure be known in other ways. They may pout, give you the silent treatment, carefully avoid topics that could engender conflict, or punish you by maintaining emotional distance. These tactics are extremely damaging to relationships. Again, it's healthier to talk about disagreements than to sweep them under the rug.

ॐ

Anger

Unfortunately, a lot of people are addicted to anger as a way of handling conflict. People who regularly explode are not healthy, nor are they happy. Again, if the relationship is worth saving, a well-trained professional counselor can help with anger management. Behavior can be changed . . . with God's help.

ॐ

[Love] is not easily angered.
1 Corinthians 13:5

Manipulation

Manipulation can take many different forms. Here are just a few:

- **Guilt:** "Now, honey, Grandma is getting very old, and you should just do as she says. She may not live much longer."

- **Flattery:** "It would be such an honor for me if someone of your significance were to do that for me."

- **Threats:** "If you don't want to accompany me to the party, I'm sure there are a lot of other women who would love to go with me."

- **Blackmail:** "If you do this, I won't tell Dad what you did with the gift he gave you."

- **Subtle deal-making:** "I know what I'm asking turns you off, but if you'll go ahead and do it, I think you'll be glad you did."

- **Blatant pay-off:** "If you'll go along with me on this one, I'll do what you want on that other one."

ॐ

How Mature Individuals Handle Conflict

- They have a strong commitment to harmony, but only if it involves openness and authenticity on the part of both individuals.

- Both persons have a deep respect for themselves and for the other individual.

- Both persons expect there to be differences between them, and they welcome them.

- They appreciate the uniqueness of the other person and understand the importance of listening and hearing accurately.

- Each has a strong sense of comfort in the relationship.

- They are determined to deal with conflict, not ignore it.

- Both are able to admit when they are wrong.

- *They are not defensive—they feel no sense of competition or the desire to win.*

- *They are both eager to congratulate one another when differences are resolved happily.*

- *They recognize that the road to love needs to be kept clear of conflict and resentment and are willing to spend the time required to get this done.*

Therefore:

Any couple who desires a lasting marriage should learn how to manage conflict constructively. Obviously the best time to determine whether two people have what it takes to keep the lines of communication open is well before settling on a wedding date. Open communication should be developed at the beginning of a relationship, rather than waiting until the last moment to unload all your baggage.

ॐ

Lifelong Commitment

It was on August 21st in the "summer of their youth" that my mom and dad committed themselves to each other. Their lifetime pledge was monumental for our family. It made possible my two sisters and me, twelve grandchildren, twelve great-grandchildren, and two great-great-grandchildren. Their commitment of undying affection to each other gave birth to a physical and emotional security that radically influenced everything about their lives—and ours—forever.

ॐ

A Look at the Vows

Take a look at the traditional wedding vows for a clear understanding of what it is you are committing to. Usually, there is a single question to which you answer "I do," and then a specific vow that you say to your mate. These few simple words will affect you for the rest of your life.

The question:

"**James,** do you take Susan to be your wife, and do you solemnly promise to love, honor, and cherish her, and that forsaking all others for her alone, you will perform unto her all the duties that a husband owes to his wife until God by death shall separate you?"

∂

The vow:

"**I,** Susan, take you, James, to be my husband. And I promise and covenant before God and these witnesses to be your loving and faithful wife—in plenty and in want, in joy and in sorrow, in sickness and in health—as long as we both shall live."

The commitment:

- Love your mate until one of you dies.
- Honor your mate until one of you dies.
- Cherish your mate until one of you dies.
- Do not be involved with any other "substitute mate."
- Perform all the duties as a spouse until one of you dies.
- Be loving and faithful through every kind of circumstance for as long as the two of you live.

Marriage is far too demanding—far too complex—to be taken on by anyone who is unsure of his or her determination to stick with a marriage partner through every challenge of life. These are radical promises! Can you honestly say to yourself, *I want to live with this person for the rest of my life?*

Questions to Consider:

- Can you ever know enough to commit yourself to another person for a lifetime?

- Is it possible to know if a particular person is the right person for you—for the rest of your life?

- Can you ever know enough at the beginning to pledge yourself to your spouse for a lifetime—no matter what happens?

- What exactly are you doing when you ask yourself whether a particular person will be the right person for you for the rest of your life?

Fundamentally, you are trying to determine whether you and the other person have what it takes to stay together. It's imperative that there be a tenacious determination to love, honor, and cherish, to perform all your duties, and to faithfully care for your mate through every kind of circumstance that may come your way. It's this kind of commitment that you must be able to pledge before getting caught up in marriage plans.

ॐ

Questions and Answers about Commitment

. **If you committed yourself when you were young and uninformed, and your marriage has been a terrible disappointment, should you live with that commitment forever?**

ॐ

Focusing on lifelong commitment changes the way people build their relationship from the very beginning. If they assume their marriage will last as long as they live, they will have a totally different attitude than if they expect to walk away if things don't work out.

· Should you remain true to your wedding vows if your mate has a problem with drugs or alcohol, has an affair, has an explosive temper, or has total disregard for you?

৵

Most of the time, a failing marriage is a symptom of problems that have little to do with the marriage itself. To make a marriage healthy, one or both partners need to do the hard work of making and keeping themselves healthy.

- However strong your willpower, can it overpower, outwit, or outwait all the problems that might occur?

ॐ

When marriages become sick, they need professional help. Sometimes two people need to be separated until they can do the therapeutic work to get healthy. But this in no way cancels the commitment they made to each other. In fact, emotional, physical, or spiritual sickness gives unconditional love the best chance to show its true character.

Benefits of Commitment

Commitment holds a couple together:

- *During the first few years.* If vows are made with seriousness, people will give their relationship a chance to develop.

- *During the flat places.* Every relationship has some periods when growth seems to stop and boredom sets in. Pledges of lifelong love are infinitely valuable during these times.

- *During relational "snags."* Most relationships go through times of trouble, but commitment to love and cherish can save a marriage.

Stability

Commitment significantly increases the feeling of permanence and stability.

When someone completely trusts in his or her mate, there is no fear of the future. Instead, there's a peaceful permanence that pervades the home and generates the glue that binds a marriage together. Children growing up in a household parented by a couple with a stable marriage have fewer behavioral problems and cope better with life's challenges.

ॐ

Trust and Intimacy

Commitment makes trust and intimacy possible. When you know in the deepest parts of your being that your marriage partner is absolutely committed to you forever, what a powerful difference that makes. A future together is assured. All your dreams and goals are possible.

Unconditional Love

Commitment helps you to soar together on the wings of unconditional love. This kind of love will provide *lift* to your relationship. You are not held together by relational successes but by a "blood covenant." This kind of covenant generates a deep inner security. It guarantees that what's yours is mine and what's mine is yours. It says that your friends are my friends and your enemies are my enemies. It says, "I will never leave you nor forsake you."

Love, Honor, and Cherish

The responsibility involved with this overwhelming commitment should be considered before you are married. Now is the time to carefully think about your relationship with this person and whether it can be sustained for a lifetime. After you make your pledge of faithfulness, your focus changes to how you can most effectively keep your commitment—how you can deeply love, honor, and cherish your mate.

ॐ

Therefore:

Don't be afraid to walk away from the relationship at any time before you say your vows—even if it's while you're standing before a minister, priest, or rabbi. It doesn't matter whether you have tickets for your honeymoon or if the ring cost more than a year's salary. If you are unsure about your pledge, don't make it. But once you have made your commitment, make it work. Be a person of your word.

Celebrate Your Marriage With Family and Friends

If a bride and groom know that all the important people in their lives are feeling deeply satisfied and pleased about their marriage, what a contribution it makes to their own sense of pleasure about what is happening! Family and friends are crucial to the health of a marriage, because they have a great deal of influence in your life.

ॐ

Should Parents and Friends Influence Mate Selection?

- The bottom line always remains the same: Every bride and groom needs to make their own decision about marriage, one they can live with for the rest of their lives.

- The wisdom of the decision depends on the depth and accuracy of their knowledge about themselves and their potential mate.

- For parents and friends, there is a fine line between being overly intrusive and being genuinely honest and helpful.

- Parents and close friends may have standards for a marriage partner that are nearly impossible to satisfy. Honest communication can help to alleviate their concerns.

- When it comes to getting married, a bride and groom need to maintain a careful balance. It's risky to marry someone just because he or she satisfies your parents. But when your family and friends tell you your potential mate is "just not right for you," it's equally unwise to ignore their opinions.

Confidence Helps Ensure Success

The enormity of selecting the right mate is almost overwhelming. This decision will radically affect everything about your existence for as long as you live. Because there is so much riding on your choice, you should be as sure as possible. The confidence you have in your decision is an essential part of a successful outcome. When you deeply believe your choice is a great one, you will trust your future marriage partner even more.

ॐ

If the people who know you best think your decision is brilliant, your confidence level will be significantly bolstered. Parents and close friends vary tremendously in their ability to help with the mate-selection decision. But take seriously the advice of all these persons. They frequently see things that need to be considered. If they find themselves unable to support your decision, they at least need to be listened to carefully and respectfully.

ॐ

Winning the Approval of Potential Stepchildren

Children from a previous marriage often have strong feelings about a potential mate for their parent. These feelings need to be handled with great sensitivity. Stepchildren can play a crucial role in determining the eventual success of a new marriage. If they are negative about their parent's choice, they can be highly destructive to the relationship. But they can be equally constructive if they have developed a positive attitude about the new family member.

ॐ

Having the full and free support of your children is of great value when you're contemplating a new marriage. This support is a goal worth working toward with patience and determination. When it's been reached, the payoff will contribute substantially to a happy marriage. The family unit will be strengthened immeasurably by the confidence your children place in your new mate.

When Your Family and Friends Object

If you are absolutely positive that you have found the person for you, but your parents or friends absolutely disagree, here are a few suggestions:

- Remain as open and receptive as you can. Remember, you have the final decision.

- Take your time! There's no hurry.

- Sit down and listen to their objections. Encourage them to tell you everything they can think of that has entered into their conclusion.

- Carefully compare their observations with your own. Be as objective as you can. Are they right about a particular point? If so, does it change your decision?

- If there are major differences between their analysis and your own, and if you are left unsure or confused, seek some help from other friends or relatives—especially those who can help you better understand your parent or friend who is concerned about you.

- Don't be afraid to seek professional counseling.

When You Are Unsure about Your Choice

What if parents and friends are certain you've made the right choice, but you're not? Don't go forward with the wedding! It doesn't matter what your parents and friends think if you're not convinced. It's you who is getting married, and you are the one who needs to be confident about your decision.

Increasing Your Chances of Success

A careful observance of each of these principles will significantly increase your odds of a lasting and satisfying marriage. To ignore any one of them is to take a substantial risk of ending up in the enormous group of people whose marriages break apart. But all the preparatory work will be worth it if you develop a loving relationship that will last a lifetime.

The Principles Are Crystal Clear

- Take your time selecting a mate.

- Develop a high degree of conscious clarity about the person you wish to marry.

- Make sure the person you marry is similar to you.

- Get married only if both of you are emotionally healthy.

- Make sure you are passionately attracted to the person you want to marry, but wait until you are married to express the full intensity of your passion.

- Decide to get married only after you have experienced a deeper, more stable kind of love.

- Develop mastery in the area of verbal intimacy.

- Learn how to resolve differences before marriage.

- Get married only when you are ready to be absolutely committed to your future partner for a lifetime.

- If your parents, relatives, and close friends support your marriage, celebrate with them! If they don't, listen carefully before you make your final decision.

ॐ

About the Author

Neil Clark Warren is one of America's best-known relational psychologists with 30 years in private practice. He holds a doctorate in clinical psychology from the University of Chicago. Currently, he is in private practice full time in the Pasadena area.

Dr. Warren is a much sought after speaker who captivates his listeners with his ability to relate complex issues in a simple, practical, and easily understood format. He has been a guest on more than 1,500 radio and television programs—and he is a frequent guest of Dr. James Dobson on Focus on the Family. He has also appeared on the Oprah Winfrey show and other national TV programs.

Dr. Warren and his wife, Marylyn, live in Southern California. They have three grown daughters.

Focus on the Family®

Welcome to the Family!

It began in 1977 with the vision of Dr. James Dobson, a licensed psychologist and author of best selling books on marriage, parenting, and family. Alarmed by the many pressures threatening the American family, he founded Focus on the Family, now an international organization dedicated to preserving family values through the life-changing message of Jesus Christ.

༜

For more information about the ministry, or if we can be of help to your family, simply write to Focus on the Family, Colorado Springs, CO 80995 or call 1-800-A-FAMILY. Friends in Canada may write to Focus on the Family, P.O. Box 9800, Stn. Terminal, Vancouver, B.C. V6B 4G3 or call 1-800-661-9800. Visit our Web site at *www.family.org*.

We'd love to hear from you!

Additional copies of this book are available at your local bookstore.

If you have enjoyed this book, or if it has
impacted your life, we would like to hear from you.
Please contact us at:

Honor Books
4050 Lee Vance View
Colorado Springs, Colorado 80918

Or visit us online at: www.cookministries.com

HONOR HB BOOKS